Routes of Cross-Cultural Exchange

Phoenician Trade Routes

Bridey Heing

Cavendish Square
New York

Published in 2018 by Cavendish Square Publishing, LLC
243 5th Avenue, Suite 136, New York, NY 10016

First Edition

CPSIA Compliance Information: Batch #CS17CSQ

All websites were available and accurate when this book was sent to press.

Library of Congress Cataloging-in-Publication Data

Names: Heing, Bridey, author.
Title: Phoenician trade routes / Bridey Heing.
Description: New York : Cavendish Square Publishing, [2018] | Series: Routes of cross-cultural exchange | Includes bibliographical references and index.
Identifiers: LCCN 2016052780 (print) | LCCN 2016054836 (ebook) | ISBN 9781502628619 (library bound) | ISBN 9781502628626 (E-book)
Subjects: LCSH: Phoenicians—Juvenile literature. | Trade routes—Mediterranean Region—History—Juvenile literature. | Mediterranean Region—History—To 476—Juvenile literature.
Classification: LCC DS81 .H37 2017 (print) | LCC DS81 (ebook) | DDC 937/.01—dc23
LC record available at https://lccn.loc.gov/2016052780

Editorial Director: David McNamara
Editor: Caitlyn Miller
Copy Editor: Michele Suchomel-Casey
Associate Art Director: Amy Greenan
Designer: Jessica Nevins
Production Coordinator: Karol Szymczuk
Photo Research: J8 Media

The photographs in this book are used by permission and through the courtesy of: Cover, De Agostini Picture Library/Getty Images; p. 5 Leemage/Universal Images Group/Getty Images; p. 8 Michael Runkel/Getty Images; p. 11 This file was provided to Wikimedia Commons by Geographicus Rare Antique Maps (http://www.g eographicus.com/), a specialist dealer in rare maps and other cartography of the 15th, 16th, 17th, 18th and 19th centuries, as part of a cooperation project/File: 1741 Homann Heirs Map of Ancient Greece ^ the Eastern Mediterranean - Geographicus - Graecia-homannheirs-1741.jpg/Wikimedia Commons/Public Domain; p. 12 CM Dixon/Print Collector/Hulton Archive/Getty Images; p. 16 Publisher New York Ward, Lock/ https://archive.org/details/illustratedhisto01newyuoft/File: Phoenician Merchants and Traders.jpg/Wikimedia Commons/Public Domain; p. 23 Anonymous (Phoenicia)/Acquired by Henry Walters, 1925, Walters Art Museum /File: Phoenician - Bowl with Hunting Scene - Walters 57705.jpg /Wikimedia Commons/CCA-SA 3.0; p. 26 Anonymous (Phoenicia)/Acquired by Henry Walters, 1929, Walters Art Museum/File: Phoenician - Crown with Goddesses and Ibexes - Walters 57968.jpg/Wikimedia Commons/Public Domain; p. 27 A. Sobkowski, own work/File: Jerycho8.jpg/Wikimedia Commons/Public Domain; p. 31 Anonymous Byzantine artist 9th century/"De Byzance a Istambul" p.129/File: Shroud of Charlemagne manufactured in Constantinople 814.jpg/Wikimedia Commons/Public Domain; p. 33 PHAS/UIG/Getty Images; pp. 38, 70 DEA/G. Dagli Orti/De Agostini/Getty Images; p. 40 Werner Forman/Universal Images Group/Getty Images; p. 45 Carole Raddato (https://www.flickr.com/people/41523983@N08) from Frankfurt, Germany/The Antelopes Fresco, from Akrotiri, Thera (Santorini), Minoan Civilization, 16th Century BC, National Archaeological Museum of Athens (https://w ww.flickr.com/photos/carolemage/14115163145/)/File: The Antelopes Fresco, from Akrotiri, Thera (Santorini), Minoan Civilization,16th Century BC, National Archaeological Museum of Athens (14115163145).jpg/Wikimedia Commons/CCA-SA 2.0 Generic; p. 48 Latitudestock/Gallo Images/Getty Images; p. 51 Koppas, Own work/File: Hittite Lion Ankara Museum Anatolian Civilizations.JPG/Wikimedia Commons/CCA-SA 3.0; p. 53 Jastrow (Own Work)/Louvre Museum/File: Relief Herodotus cour Carree Louvre.jpg/Wikimedia Commons/CCA 3.0 Unported; p. 56 Danita Delimont/Gallo Images/Getty Images; p. 63 canan kaya/Shutterstock.com; p. 72 Ludmiła Pilecka, Own work/File: Ruins of Carthage.jpg/Wikimedia Commons/CCA 3.0 Unported; p. 74 Brigida Soriano/Shutterstock.com; p. 77 Peter Dennis/Getty Images; p. 78 Daderot, Own work/File: Striding Lion 1 from Processional Way in Babylon, Neo-Babylonian Period, c. 604-562 BC, molded and glazed brick – Oriental Institute Museum, University of Chicago - DSC07255.JPG/Wikimedia Commons/Creative Commons CC0 1.0 Public Domain Dedication; p. 79 Siamax, Own work/File: Olympic Park Cyrus.jpg /Wikimedia Commons/CCA-SA 3.0 Unported; pp. 82-83 Milonk/Shutterstock.com.

Printed in the United States of America

Table of Contents

Introduction

Powering the Ancient World Through Trade

Trade has been a key way for people to share culture, goods, and ideas throughout human history. In the ancient world, where communication and travel were limited, trade was even more important. It was through trade that **civilizations** were able to communicate and learn from and about each other. Traders pushed mankind forward as they exchanged products, currency, and skills. For centuries, the Phoenicians were leaders in **cross-cultural** trade. They connected the Mediterranean and western Asia through their commercial networks and shaped the civilizations of their time.

Phoenicia was a group of **city-states** along the eastern coast of the Mediterranean, focused around modern Lebanon and Syria. The cities of Phoenicia were independent but had a cultural identity that linked them together. Phoenicia is believed to have been established in 1500 BCE and lasted until 539 BCE, when Persian Cyrus the Great conquered it.

The Phoenicians were skilled at building ships, as shown by this carving found on the side of a sarcophagus in the ancient city of Sidon.

In the one thousand years Phoenicia was independent, it established trade routes that were extremely influential. The Phoenicians traded by sea and by land. Their routes stretched to Greece, Mesopotamia, and India. These routes were for both export and import, allowing merchants to serve as a connection between the Eastern and Western ancient worlds. The important role they played is clear in the art, writings, and accounts of the many empires and cultures with which they interacted. Phoenicia is mentioned in the works of Homer and the Bible and seen in art in Arabia.

Trade was the basis of Phoenicia's economy, and it made the Phoenicians very wealthy. Some of Phoenicia's earliest trade was with Greece, where Phoenicia's Tyrian purple dye was used by elites in their clothing. Over the course of centuries, Phoenician merchants became the era's most successful traders. Dye would remain one of their most important exports, along with cedar wood and glass. Phoenicians also traded in silver and tin. They brought these two metals from Spain and other western ports to the East to be mixed with copper to make bronze. They also traded in wine, pottery, food, animals, and papyrus, among other goods.

But it wasn't just goods that Phoenicians brought through their trade routes. Phoenicia was the first civilization to develop a **phonetic** alphabet, which they used in their trade business and quickly spread to other parts of the world. The development of a phonetic alphabet was a major step in the evolution of writing, which had been based on hieroglyphic-like symbols rather than individual letters. The Greek alphabet is based on it, meaning that all European alphabets (which are based on the Greek alphabet) are part of the Phoenician trade legacy.

Trade routes served another purpose as well: helping Phoenicia establish colonies. While Greece dominated the northern Mediterranean, Phoenicia controlled the south and set up trade posts along its routes. These eventually grew into colonies, many of which still exist as modern cities, such as Tripoli in Libya, Palermo in Sicily, and Ibiza in Spain. One of the most influential was Carthage, in what is now Tunisia in North Africa. Carthage developed into an empire, fought wars with Greece and Syracuse, and eventually fell to the Roman Empire. It was rebuilt by Julius Caesar and became one of the Roman Empire's largest cities and an influential center of Christianity.

Although little is known about Phoenician culture outside of trade, its legacy makes clear how important trade routes were to the ancient world. These pathways between cultures were the primary way that civilizations advanced, made peace, learned, and communicated—all at a time when travel was incredibly difficult and dangerous. The Phoenician trade routes were among the most advanced of their time, making the small Phoenician coastal civilization one of the guiding forces of the ancient world. For over one thousand years, Phoenicia was a link between East and West, connecting far-flung empires and cultures to create a business empire.

In this book, we will explore the way Phoenicians established their trade routes, how those routes were used to influence the ancient world, and what legacy Phoenicia left behind. We will discuss the goods, ideas, and people who made Phoenician trade routes some of the most important in their time, the challenges merchants faced, and what became of the trade routes as history went on.

Trade has always been about more than business—it shapes our culture and history. For Phoenicia, that meant playing a role in some of the greatest empires mankind has ever known.

Chapter 1

Trade Before the Phoenicians

The Phoenicians revolutionized trade in their time, but they were not the first major traders in the ancient world. In the early Bronze Age, regional trade arose in the Mediterranean, Near East, and China. Increased trade helped establish trade routes that would eventually become the legendary Silk Road and would bridge the Roman Empire and the Far East. In the Mediterranean, the Minoans established a network that gave way to the Phoenicians' routes, connecting Egypt to Greece and the Levant to Sicily. In the Middle East, trade led to the growth of the Assyrian Empire, which became one of the strongest empires of its time. Smaller-scale trade also spread across China and India, eventually reaching Egypt and west Africa.

Opposite: *Before the Late Bronze Age Collapse, the Minoans were the dominant traders in the Mediterranean. This Minoan fresco was excavated on Knossos.*

What set the Phoenicians apart from the trade routes and merchants who came before them was their ability to overcome a few common barriers. The Phoenicians developed a type of ship that featured a curved hull, which helped them withstand the rough waters of the Mediterranean Sea. They were also able to use their small size to their advantage. Phoenicians also lacked **imperial aspirations** and made lasting peace with neighboring civilizations that might otherwise have sought to conquer them. Although the Persians eventually did set out to dominate the Phoenicians (and they ultimately succeeded), for centuries Phoenicians were able to build wealth through trade as few **mercantile** civilizations had before. In this chapter, we will learn about some of the significant traders before the Phoenicians and what obstacles the Phoenicians mastered before becoming the leading traders of their time.

Major Trade Networks

Before the Phoenicians, Mediterranean trade was dominated by the Minoans of Crete. Little is known about this civilization due to a lack of decipherable language. However, we do know that the Minoans established the earliest civilization in Europe and built the continent's first palace at Knossos. The Minoans are believed to have emerged around 3650 BCE and flourished for the next two thousand years.

The Minoans established a large network of trade throughout the Mediterranean Sea, stretching from Greece to Egypt to the Near East. Their trade routes were similar in scope to the Phoenicians', including land and sea routes. These routes also allowed the

This 1741 map shows the Mediterranean at the time of the ancient Greeks. Phoenicia lies along the eastern edge of the Mediterranean.

Minoans to influence cultures throughout the ancient world. Along with goods like copper, saffron, and papyrus, the Minoans influenced ceramic arts and jewelry. They also facilitated the exchange of culture and ideas between Egypt and Greece. In turn, the Minoans saw those two powerful civilizations' influence on the island of Crete, where the power of the Minoans was focused.

Between 1700 BCE and 1100 BCE, natural disasters and the rise of the Greeks brought about the end of the Minoan period. It is believed that earthquakes in 1700 BCE and 1450 BCE led to widespread destruction from which the Minoans didn't recover. Shortly after 1450 BCE, in around 1420 BCE,

Mycenaean Greeks conquered Minoan strongholds and castles. Despite continued existence in some city-states, the Minoan civilization declined until it is believed to have ended completely in 1100 BCE.

In the East, caravan routes were established to facilitate trade throughout China around 2000 BCE. These routes were primarily used to trade precious stones, such as jade. There is also evidence that trade was possible with civilizations as far west as Egypt, where Chinese silk has been found. In the Middle East, the Assyrians were the dominant traders of the region. They set up trading posts in Anatolia during the twentieth century BCE, where they traded tin, copper, and clothing in exchange for gold and silver. Karum Kanesh, one of the trade cities established by the Assyrians, grew to be one of the most important centers of commerce in its age. The city fed wealth

These sculptures sat at the entrance to the Assyrian palace of Khorsabad. The Assyrians were a Middle Eastern empire to which Phoenicia paid tribute.

back to the growing Assyrian Empire. Trade with Anatolia, which is now modern Turkey, also provided the Assyrians with iron to fashion weapons. The empire flourished in part due to its complex banking system, which was established to help manage the wealth it gained through trade.

The Assyrians also traded frequently with Iran, or Persia, maintaining their trade routes until around the fourteenth century BCE. Then rival traders challenged their dominance in the Mediterranean and the rivers to the Persian Gulf. During this time, India traded primarily with China to the east and with west Africa to the west and did not develop a significant **maritime** trade presence until around 600 BCE.

Obstacles to Trade Before the Phoenicians

Trade was widespread and complex for around one thousand years before the Phoenicians became prominent. Yet there were many dangers and concerns that made trade difficult. Mastering these obstacles was part of what allowed the Phoenicians to become so powerful and for their trade routes to become stable enough to spread goods, services, and culture.

The first concern was the Mediterranean Sea itself. The rough waters of the Mediterranean were dangerous and unpredictable, putting trade ships and the goods they carried at risk. But the Phoenicians developed ships that could stand up to the choppy waters, featuring curved hulls, back-heavy designs, sails that could be shifted to catch changing winds, and protected spaces for delicate and valuable cargo. They also sailed close to the shore and during the day, which gave rise to the number of colonies and trade posts that eventually grew into cities in their own right.

The second obstacle the Phoenicians overcame was war. The city-states that made up the Phoenician civilization were located in a small area along the eastern edge of the Mediterranean, with major empires on all sides. Yet the Phoenicians leveraged their trade to build alliances and establish themselves as useful, making the idea of conquering them less appealing. Although they had some conflicts with the Greeks in the northern Mediterranean, the Phoenicians were largely able to work out arrangements with all their neighbors that allowed them to carry out their important trade without threat. This is due in part to the value of what they traded, be it dye and copper or wood and tin. These were goods that were not available through other means, making the Phoenicians crucial middlemen.

Sargon the Great

Sargon the Great was one of the early kings of Assyria. Under his rule the civilization began its journey toward becoming an empire. He conquered ancient Mesopotamia, becoming one of the first rulers to control an empire with centralized power. Little is known for sure about Sargon the Great. There is not much textual evidence about his reign, and a number of legends that he and his successors built around him make it difficult to separate out the truth from his boasts. We do know that he claimed power in a possible **coup**, established or rebuilt the city of Akkad, and from there raised a military that he used to create his empire. He held power from 2334 BCE to 2279 BCE. During that time he used the stability of his empire to expand trade. Sargon is believed to have established the first agreements to set up *karum*, or trade posts, in Anatolia. The wealth provided by trade with Anatolia helped strengthen the Assyrian military and government, giving rise to complex banking systems and trade practices. Under Sargon the Great, measures were made uniform for use in trade and a postal system was established. According to legend, ships may have also made contact with India. The central strength of Assyria under Sargon the Great was what allowed for such expansion, and trade was what gave the empire stability.

Chapter 2

Foundations and Explorations

Phoenicia was one of the most influential civilizations of its time. Despite this, our understanding of the Phoenicians is largely determined by others' descriptions, such as writings by the Greeks. These writings are a testament to the importance of Phoenician trade. And this trade shaped both the Phoenicians and the empires with which they traded. Without trade, the small civilization could have disappeared in history and the empires bound for fame could have looked very different. Trade allowed the Phoenicians to spread culture and ideas along with goods and materials. Their importance as merchants is reflected in their role in the cultures they helped shape. From the iconic purple dye they provided to the Greeks to the metals needed to make copper, the impact of Phoenician traders is still relevant today. Even the

Opposite: *This painting shows a busy Phoenician port, where merchants and traders from around the world bought and sold goods and exchanged information.*

name "Phoenicia" speaks to their role as traders. It comes from the Greek word *Phoinikes*, a reference to the purple dye Phoenician traders brought to the empire.

In this chapter, we will learn how the Phoenicians became a trading power. We will read about the rise of Phoenicia and the evolution of their trade routes. We will also discuss the role of technology in the spread of trade, what trade meant to their civilization, and the ways in which the Phoenicians carried out trade with differing communities, including imports and exports.

The Rise of Phoenicia

The civilization we now know as Phoenicia, called Canaan during its own time, was a collection of **Semitic** city-states that had some independence in politics and culture. Phoenicia was centered around modern Lebanon, sitting on the northern coast of the Middle East. There is evidence that the city of Sidon, which became one of the most powerful cities in Phoenicia, was established around 4000 BCE. Other Phoenician cities followed afterward. By 3200 BCE, these cities were stable enough to begin forming the alliances that would become Phoenicia. Some had already established trade relations with other civilizations by that point. The city-states retained their **hereditary monarchies**. However, the merchant classes were very powerful, and many city-states followed similar policies to maintain cooperation. Cultural and religious similarities were the true binding powers between city-states, rather than formal political ties.

Phoenicia was fully established by 2750 BCE, with the cities of Tyre and Sidon as the centers of power and trade. Byblos and Baalbek served as religious centers. Tyre eventually replaced Sidon as the economic power of Phoenicia, partially because it was the home of Tyrian dye. For most city-states, their role in trade determined their size and importance.

In 1200 BCE, the Sea Peoples are believed to have invaded or migrated into the area. The Sea Peoples are a little understood group of possibly European or Anatolian tribes that began attacking Egypt in the fourteenth century BCE. The name "Sea Peoples" originated in the 1800s, when Egyptian tablets were found detailing war with attackers described as being of or from the sea. Although little is known about them, evidence of interaction between the Phoenicians and the Sea Peoples was found at Byblos. Around 1200 BCE, the Sea Peoples are believed to have destroyed other Levant cities while sparing those city-states that were part of Phoenicia. The reason for this isn't known, but it is believed to have given rise to a sharing of maritime technology and corresponds to the rise of Phoenician trade posts and colonies.

In 1200 BCE, Phoenicia's position as a leading trade civilization was bolstered by a mysterious disaster that befell many neighboring empires. Between 1200 and 1150, the Egyptians, Anatolians, Hittites, and Mycenaeans in Greece suffered near or complete destruction. Numerous cities were destroyed, economies floundered, and trade was disrupted. A dark age of sorts followed, lasting for a few centuries as civilizations recovered. This downturn is called the Late Bronze Age Collapse. It is believed to have been caused by climate change, natural disaster, or war that led to the failure of systems and institutions that had been holding up those civilizations. Phoenicia did not suffer this collapse. Through trade its people helped revive the regional economy.

In the 800s BCE, Phoenicia was conquered by a series of larger empires, which caused its influence to decline. Beginning in 883 BCE with the invasion of the Assyrians, Phoenicia was never again independent. Control of the area—and the seafaring tradition the people had developed—passed from Assyria to Babylon to Persia before moving into the Classical period, with Greek and Roman dominance. The area that was Phoenicia would remain under imperial and colonial rule until 1943, when it was granted independence from France as modern-day Lebanon.

The Spread of Trade

Trade was already a key part of the regional economy when the Phoenicians were developing their routes. But prior to the Phoenicians, trade was largely regional and did not stretch so far as the trade routes eventually would. The Phoenicians tapped into established routes and expanded them through innovation. They also used the lack of a central trade leader in the aftermath of the Late Bronze Age Collapse to their advantage. The Phoenicians had outposts throughout the Mediterranean and strong trade relations with empires in the ancient world. Thus, they positioned themselves as the sole source of key goods, including wood, glass, and cloth. The trade routes made Phoenician merchants wealthy and powerful.

The routes also shaped and strengthened the cultures and economies of the empires with which they traded.

The Phoenicians began establishing their trade networks around 1500 BCE. At that point, trade was primarily with the Greeks, to whom the Phoenicians sold Tyrian dye used in the clothing of elites. It was this exchange that eventually led to the association of the color purple with royalty, as it was a rare and valuable pigment favored by leadership. Following the Egyptian decline of 1200 BCE, the Phoenicians expanded their westward trading. They established colonies and trade ports along northern Africa and opened trade relations with more far-flung allies.

Phoenician trade routes spread from the eastern coast of the Mediterranean to the Atlantic. There is some evidence that trade ships made the journey to Britain and the Canary Islands. However, it is still unclear if these kinds of long-haul journeys took place. Routes stayed close to the coast, running north along Asia Minor to Crete and southwest along the entire coast of North Africa. Routes also cut north to Sardinia and Sicily, as well as Iberia, or modern Spain. Although known best for their sea trade, Phoenicians also traded with India and Asian civilizations via land routes that connected China to the Mediterranean.

Between 1500 BCE and 300 BCE, Phoenician trade is believed to have been at its height. The Phoenicians set up cities along the Mediterranean, including Carthage in 814 BCE and Tingis at the Strait of Gibraltar in the fifth century BCE. The exact date that many of these city-states were established is debated. This is due in part to the fact that many started as way stations for traders. They were set up roughly a one-day journey from one another. Some had more sophisticated facilities, and others were little more than stopping-off points. Phoenicians also established secondary production sites for dye and other valued goods, cutting the amount of time it took to get these goods to the farther reaches of their trade network.

These ports played multiple roles in maintaining Phoenician trade dominance. By cutting the journey into smaller, more easily managed increments, sailors and traders could make journeys safely and stop off without using non-Phoenician ports. Phoenicians also used these city-states as production sites, as they did with their Tyrian dye in modern-day Morocco. Additionally, ports served as a way to ensure Phoenician traders were not caught off guard by rivals. Ports potentially served as military outposts should enemies attempt to take control of the trade routes.

Some of the trading posts the Phoenicians established went on to become major cities, including Tripoli in Libya. Carthage is today known as Tunis (the capital of Tunisia) and played a significant role in the ancient world after the fall of Phoenician dominance. The Phoenician system of city-states with loose affiliation meant that these outposts grew and evolved independently. Therefore, when Phoenicia was conquered, these city-states continued to exist—separate from the civilization that founded them.

Technology and Trade

Technology played a significant role in Phoenician trade strength, including their uniquely designed ships and the goods they made that were sold around the ancient world. Given the lack of primary source

Phoenician goods, like this bowl, were highly prized for their quality and artistry. This one shows a hunting scene with Egyptian and Mesopotamian elements.

evidence available about the Phoenicians, we don't have a full understanding of how many innovations are original to their culture. But we do know that they made expert use of mathematics, navigation, and new ship designs. Their use of existing technology and their improvements to that technology made it possible for them to develop advanced trade routes.

Trade Ships and Coastal Navigation

Ships were among the most important technological advancements for the Phoenicians. Their ships were stronger, sturdier, and more developed for trade. Phoenicians also designed specialized warships, which featured multiple sails and a narrower build than their trade ships. The bow of warships was outfitted with bronze so that the ship itself could be used as a weapon by ramming enemy ships.

But it was Phoenician trade ships that were truly revolutionary and let this small civilization become the maritime power of its age. Trading ships were called *galloi* by the Greeks and were round in shape. The hulls and sides were curved, and the ship itself was squat, allowing it to rest high in the water rather than sinking low. An oar on the left side of the ship was used to steer, while a sail that hung loosely enough to change direction allowed the ship to catch the wind as needed. The storage space near the rear of the ship weighted it for stability and featured insulation that protected delicate goods like glass or ceramic from the rough journey on the Mediterranean's choppy waters.

Navigation was another area where the Phoenicians developed huge innovations. On short journeys, they used coastal navigation, which was made possible by the design of their trade ships. By keeping the coast in sight, Phoenicians could track progress and maintain a sense of position. They were safer there, too, due to the difficult-to-navigate, rockier terrain nearer the coast. The Phoenicians also made use of the night sky when navigating on longer journeys. In fact, the North Star was once called the Phoenician Star because of the star's role in their navigation. Celestial navigation would become one of the standard methods for deep-sea navigation. It helped the Phoenicians safely explore the west Mediterranean and the Atlantic.

Innovating the Alphabet

The alphabet invented by the Phoenicians also played a significant role in their trade, providing uniform documentation and measures for goods. Around 1200 BCE the alphabet was developed. At that time, most forms of writing were hieroglyphics, which use symbols to stand for whole words rather than sounds. The phonetic nature of the alphabet made it simple to learn and use across languages. The Phoenician alphabet was eventually the basis of other alphabets that followed, such as Hebrew and Arabic. In addition to letters, the Phoenicians developed **numerals** similar to Roman numerals up to the number 9. Glyphs were used to denote higher values. This simple glyph system also used multiplication to signify values beyond 10, 20, and 100 (which each had its own symbol). This made it possible to easily track payment and inventory.

The Nature of Phoenician Trade

Trade in the ancient world was a difficult undertaking, but it also served many purposes. For civilizations like Phoenicia, with no agriculture, it served as the basis of their economies. But it also solidified alliances and provided routes of cross-cultural communication. Some exchanges were comprised of gifts designed to reinforce demand for products or to pay tribute to foreign city-states and leaders. Phoenician trade involved all of these motivations. It drove the business and culture of its region for centuries.

Most trade conducted by the Phoenicians was established by agreements that set prices and goods

Phoenician city-states were ruled by kings. This crown belonged to the ruler of an unknown regional city in the tenth century BCE.

that were to be traded between states. Agreements included setting up trade centers. State officials were likely involved in all areas of trade. Yet trade was often conducted by merchants and traders, a class that was influential and high ranking in Phoenician society.

While the value of goods was fixed, trade wasn't necessarily done with money in the ancient world. Gold and silver were common forms of payment, but so were in-kind goods. This meant that in exchange for a decided amount of any given product, the buyer would provide a decided amount of another product or many products. For example, an Egyptian trade agreement provided seven cedar logs in exchange for gold, silver, linen, rope, lentils, fish, papyrus, and cow hides.

Phoenician trade routes were used for a variety of imports and exports. The routes were used to trade goods between trade partners, such as between Greece and Egypt or Iberia and Mesopotamia. Phoenicians were master craftsmen and used the routes to bring their own goods to their partners. Routes were also used to import products that the mainland city-states and colonies or outposts needed.

The scope of Phoenician trade, stretching from Asia to the Atlantic, made it possible to use supply and demand to its advantage. For example, papyrus or fine linen, which was available in abundance in Egypt, was of higher value in other parts of the world. This made trade a very lucrative industry for the Phoenicians. They made large financial gains on most products. Each long journey meant that trade could be conducted on both legs of the trip.

Ancient Entrepreneurs

The Phoenicians became the leading maritime traders of the ancient world for many reasons. The Phoenicians' skills at sea played a large role in their growth, but it doesn't alone explain their rise. The Late Bronze Age Collapse provided an opportunity not just for trade but also for expansion. This allowed the Phoenicians to create a network of city-states and outposts that aided their trading vessels to safely journey through the Mediterranean. The expansive nature of their trade routes also played a role. Phoenicians were vitally important to many empires that otherwise did not have access to the goods the Phoenicians were able to reliably provide. Finally, technology and innovation helped them develop new, efficient practices that kept their trade ships safe on journeys and made tracking of cargo or payment reliable.

The Phoenicians also demonstrated the relationship between trade and culture. Because of the Phoenicians, the alphabet developed and some of the most iconic symbolism of the ancient world—such as purple representing royalty—was solidified. The cross-cultural influence the Phoenicians made possible can be seen in architecture, literature, and archaeological finds. The importance of the Phoenicians in the ancient world is also demonstrated in their depictions in the works of Homer, the Bible, Egyptian tombs, and frescoes across Mesopotamia and Greece. Despite our lack of first-hand accounts, these depictions give us a sense of the role this ancient civilization played in its own world and allows its influence to live on among the many cultures it touched and shaped.

Cities like Jericho, the ruins of which are shown here, would have done frequent trade with nearby Phoenicia.

James B. Pritchard

One of the greatest challenges to understanding the Phoenicians is our lack of primary evidence about their way of life. We rely largely on Greek, Egyptian, or Mesopotamian writings about the civilization's role in ancient history. These sources have provided us with a lot of information but left a lot of gaps in our knowledge. However, we do have some first-hand knowledge of the way Phoenicians lived, traded, and worshipped, thanks in large part to American archaeologist James B. Pritchard. Pritchard specialized in excavating and studying Jordan, Israel, and Lebanon, where Phoenician city-states were most heavily clustered.

From 1964 to 1967, Pritchard worked in the Jordan Valley. There he discovered connections between the Phoenicians and the Sea Peoples, as well as Tell es-Sa'idiyeh's role as a meeting place of cultures. From 1969 to 1974, Pritchard's last excavation took place at Sarafand in Lebanon, where he discovered Sarepta, a large Phoenician city. The city is mentioned in numerous ancient texts, including the Bible under the name Zarepeth. Although not one of the major trade centers, it is one of the largest former Phoenician city sites that is not currently inhabited. This made it possible to excavate large stretches of space without disrupting an existing city. Pritchard's discoveries at Sarepta expanded our understanding of Phoenician religion, pottery work, and day-to-day life. The excavation was cut short by the Lebanese Civil War. Similarly, his excavation at Tell es-Sa'idiyeh was cut short by the Six Days' War. Yet his discoveries broadened our understanding of ancient Phoenicia.

Chapter 3

Goods and Services

The Phoenicians became master traders through many means, including technology and the economic landscape of their time. However, their trading success was due in large part to what they traded. Phoenicians diversified the goods that were transported between places. From wine to wood, they were skilled at identifying a need and filling it with efficiency and reliability.

While many of the goods the Phoenicians traded were raw materials, they also handled processed goods and styled artworks. Ceramics and glass were just two of the areas in which Phoenicians developed strong craftsmanship. Thus, the items they produced were valuable throughout the known world. Papyrus and linen were also goods transported by the Phoenicians. They sold this expensive cargo to places where it was scarce.

Opposite: *Tyrian dye, shown here on a shroud, was one of the most prized goods produced by Phoenicia. It came to symbolize royalty.*

Along with tangible goods, the Phoenicians used their trade routes to facilitate cross-cultural exchange as well. This included the Phoenician alphabet, artistic styles, and goods that took on special significance over time, such as Tyrian dye. Phoenicians themselves were also influential. They appeared in literature and art across the regions where they traded. Phoenicians were woven so tightly into the fabric of their times that the ancient Mediterranean story cannot fully be told without including them.

Slavery

While much of the Phoenician trade was positive, there was a dark side. Slavery was the norm in the ancient world. It provided a workforce that built cities and temples or otherwise provided labor for the growing empires of the time. Phoenician ships transported slaves around the Mediterranean, many of whom were captured by the Phoenicians. Phoenicians were known for kidnapping people and selling them as slaves. Others were captured as spoils of war or sold by citizens of their own cities during economic hardship.

Exported Goods

In addition to developing revolutionary seafaring skills, the Phoenicians produced high-quality, precisely made goods that became highly valued around the ancient world. The land under Phoenician control was not ideal for agriculture. Yet there were crops that grew, including olives and figs. The land was also rich in cedar trees, which were ideal for timber. A great deal of lumber was sold to Egypt and Mesopotamia, where

Phoenicians were skilled at making glass goods, like this vase from some time between the sixth and fourth centuries BCE. Colored glass was rare and highly prized.

trees were rare and thus more valuable. Phoenician traders transported the tree trunks whole, a massive and heavy undertaking that signals the kind of large-scale trade that defined the Phoenicians.

Phoenicians also became the leading producers of glass during their time, replacing the Egyptians in the field. Glass vessels, plates, mirrors, and other goods were made at Sarepta, Tyre, and Sidon, as well as adornments for jewelry or clothing. The Phoenicians also made transparent glass and may have been the first to do so. Their elaborate glass products featured near-transparent colored glass layered and shaped to make patterns. Glass goods produced in Phoenicia were traded around the world, and their methods were adopted by other civilizations. Other luxury goods, made from cedar, ivory, or gold, were also popular throughout the region.

The dye that Phoenicians sold to the Greeks was undoubtedly one of the most influential and famous goods they traded. Tyrian dye, which originated in the island city of Tyre, was made with the crushed shells of murex shellfish. In order to make the dye, fishermen had to set traps deep in the waters of the Mediterranean. Then they left thousands of the shellfish in the sun to dry. The dye was extracted from the crushed shells. The species of shellfish that was used for the dye almost became extinct due to heavy harvesting, giving a glimpse of how popular dyed clothing was.

Textiles also made up a significant portion of the exports from Phoenicia, but in a unique way. Raw materials like wool, linen yarn, and silk were brought to Phoenicia from Damascus, Persia, and Egypt to be processed and turned into clothing or carpets. Although purple was one of the most well-known colors the Phoenicians worked in, they were known for making brightly colored and patterned goods that were highly valued. Phoenician textiles made their way into art and myth.

Wine was another significant commodity traded by the Phoenicians. Phoenician city-states like Sidon and Tyre were among the most skilled winemakers of their time. They also established vineyards in colonies like Carthage. Phoenicians traded in grapevines and knowledge, allowing other cultures to develop their own winemaking traditions. As wine took on religious and cultural importance around 1000 BCE, Phoenician winemaking became all the more important and lucrative.

Imported Goods

Phoenician colonies and city-states also imported goods for use domestically or for processing. Copper, silver, and gold were all brought by ship from overseas to make the ornate artistic works for which Phoenicia was famous. Ivory, ebony, and amber were imported for use in jewelry. Foodstuffs, like grain and honey, were brought in from nearby civilizations. Although Phoenicia was rich in cedar, it also imported oak to make oars for its fleets of ships.

In addition to the strong seafaring trade tradition the Phoenicians developed, their markets were a site of much activity. Imported precious stones, farm animals, perfumes, and spices were sold on land. Phoenicia rested at the meeting point of Mediterranean trade routes and land routes through Asia. This location made it an important hub of trade and market activity where East met West. As market centers, city-states flourished and grew, and merchants became increasingly wealthy and powerful.

Phoenician colonies and outposts served a purpose for imported and exported goods as well. With colonies set up across the region, Phoenician merchants tapped into local markets and industries to facilitate trade between city-states. They also set up outposts for production of glass, dye, and wine, increasing the Phoenician capacity for output while cutting travel times significantly. These kinds of innovations helped Phoenician traders stay on the cutting edge of commerce.

Cultural Influence

While the economic impact of Phoenician trade is part of what shaped the ancient world, traders also brought items of cultural significance. Goods the Phoenicians transported became **status symbols**, influencing the way cultures interpreted wealth and luxury. Their wine changed the way people worshipped and ate. And their artistic products influenced styles that became iconic among the Greeks and Egyptians. They also facilitated cross-cultural exchanges between the civilizations with which they traded. This made it possible for peoples to influence one another without ever meeting.

We've discussed the importance of Tyrian dye at length, as both one of the main commodities the Phoenicians traded and as a luxury good in the ancient world. Tyrian dye's unique shade of red-purple became a marker of the elites, who used the dye to color sashes and clothing. Purple as a symbol of royalty lived on long after the Phoenician trade routes stopped being the sole source of the dye. It was mentioned in the Bible and remained highly linked to royalty for centuries. The dye became part of Roman and European culture as such.

Wine also took on religious importance throughout the ancient world. For the Phoenicians, wine became one of the primary goods they produced and traded. They were one of the first cultures to embrace winemaking. Therefore, they were perfectly placed to spread that knowledge and their techniques. Shortly after wine was being traded regularly throughout the ancient world, it became linked to **deities** and religious rituals. Wine was also used as an offering to honor leaders, making it highly valued. Thus, wine was very lucrative for the Phoenicians while also shaping religious rituals across ancient faiths and modern religions, including Christianity.

Phoenician art was similarly influential, and it highlights the give-and-take relationship between cultures in the ancient world. Phoenician artworks were prized in the ancient world, due to their high level of craftsmanship and advanced techniques used to add color or pattern to the work. The quality of Phoenician art is mentioned in written works from across the ancient world. Traders from Phoenicia are represented in frescoes and carvings as well. Through its colonies, Phoenician art styles were introduced to varied continents and parts of the Mediterranean.

Phoenician art, however, was also influenced by those with whom they traded. Egyptian, Greek, and Mesopotamian influence has been seen in Phoenician carvings and artworks. Although Phoenicians are often thought of as a source of influence, they too were shaped and changed by the cross-cultural communication their trade made possible.

One of the most significant cultural influences of the Phoenicians was the spread of their alphabet. Along with the way it changed trade, the introduction of a more easily learned and used alphabet made

The Phoenician alphabet was one of the first phonetic alphabets in existence and radically changed access to reading and writing.

reading and writing possible for classes that traditionally were unable to. In turn, literacy led to changes in the class structure of cultures in the Mediterranean. However, many cultures simply did not use Phoenician or Phoenician-influenced alphabets for writing at the highest levels of government, keeping governance out of the realm of the people. Cultures around the ancient world adapted the alphabet for their own languages, eventually giving rise to modern alphabets and scripts.

Phoenician Religion

In the ancient world, religion, art, and culture were all closely linked. Most artworks were created in a religious context, whether as part of religious rituals or on goods depicting religious scenes or deities. Much of the art we have from Phoenicia is based in religion, and their religious representations were tightly interwoven with trade. Their ships were decorated with images of deities and religious symbols, and temples were built across Phoenicia. Priests and religious leaders were among the most powerful people in Phoenicia. Many were part of the royal classes. Some of the strongest city-states in Phoenicia were sites of religious importance, such as Byblos.

Although we do not have a central religious work to inform our understanding of the Phoenicians' faith, we do know a great deal about their religion. Phoenician mythology is **polytheistic**, with a central, all-powerful deity named El. Other deities included Baal, Astarte, and Eshmun. All had specific roles and powers to which the Phoenicians paid homage. There is some indication that Phoenician gods influenced the way Greeks interpreted their faith, including the god Zeus.

Phoenicians worshipped in temples built solely for the purpose of honoring specific deities, much as they did in Greece or Egypt. Each deity had unique ways that followers could honor him or her. However, sacrifices and offerings were common across all temples, as were prayers and incense. Sacrifices did sometimes include humans, although to a lesser degree than ancient Roman or biblical accounts claim.

Chapter 4

The Major Players

As we've seen, trade in the ancient world was made up of many cultures and civilizations, and each was distinct. The Phoenicians grew into a trading power at a unique time in ancient history, spanning both the Bronze Age and the Iron Age. The Phoenicians' trade partners also experienced unique circumstances, including the Late Bronze Age Collapse. Some of the greatest civilizations of the ancient world (like the Mesopotamians, Greeks, and Egyptians) were still evolving into the prominent cultures we study today while they traded with the Phoenicians.

In this chapter, we will learn more about the civilizations the Phoenicians encountered and traded with. We will also look at some of the leaders in Phoenicia who had a significant impact on trade and at the role of merchants and traders in the ancient world.

Opposite: *The sarcophagus of King Ahiram contains the oldest known example of the Phoenician alphabet, dated to 1000 BCE.*

Traders in the Ancient World

Social classes were deeply engrained in the ancient world, with religious leaders and royalty at the top of the **hierarchy**. Because of limited access to education and power, there were not many opportunities for someone from one social class to enter another. Ancient civilizations were also defined by extremes: the immense wealth of the ruling classes was at one end of the social spectrum and the extremely difficult lives of slaves was at the other. But that was less true for merchants or traders, who were the central economic forces of their time. Trade was the cornerstone of the ancient economy. Those employed in trade were capable of making large fortunes. It wasn't always simple, though. Trade came with immense risk, and all could be lost very quickly with one shipwreck. In some places, such as Greece, the trading class was also made up largely of foreigners, which further complicated their place in the social structure.

Merchants and traders in the ancient Mediterranean were among what we'd today call the middle class. They were still removed from power but had the means to live more comfortably than those of lower social status. In Phoenicia, merchants and traders were second in influence only to kings and priests. Alternatively, in Greece and Egypt, they were wealthy and influential but still outside of very strictly governed **bureaucracies**. Because power itself was very firmly held by kings and priests, those outside of that sphere could influence culture or win favor with rulers. Yet people with minor influence played only an indirect role in shaping their civilizations' policies.

Phoenicia

Phoenicia was made up of many independent city-states, meaning that there were many differences between the governance and culture of each individual city. But there were also many similarities that defined them as one culture. These included artistic styles, religion, and language. There were also a few kings who ruled individual city-states in a way that shaped Phoenician culture and trade more broadly.

Hiram I is considered to be one of the most important kings in Phoenician history. Our knowledge of his reign is tightly woven with religious teachings. He ruled Tyre from 980 BCE to 947 BCE, and it was under his rule that the city-state became the most important in Phoenicia. Before Hiram I's reign began, Tyre was secondary to Sidon, another important city-state. Hiram I established strong trade relations with the kings of Israel, including the legendary King Solomon. Through trade, Hiram I became extremely wealthy. He made Tyre one of the trade centers of Phoenicia, based largely on Tyrian dye.

Another king of Tyre who was historically significant was Pygmalion, who ruled Tyre from 831 BCE to 785 BCE. Pygmalion established numerous colonies, including Kition on Cyprus and Sardinia. He also played a role in the founding of Carthage in 814 BCE, which went on to be one of the most influential capitals of the ancient world. Although the exact circumstances of the founding of Carthage are unknown, legend holds that Dido, the sister of Pygmalian, fled Tyre and founded Carthage in exile. She and the kingdom she built around Carthage feature heavily in Greek and Roman myth, including works by Virgil.

Though we do not know exactly when the Phoenician alphabet was created, it is first seen on the sarcophagus of King Ahiram, who ruled Byblos around 1000 BCE. His tomb was found in 1923 by French archaeologist Pierre Montet. The inscription on the sarcophagus is believed to be a curse against those who would disturb the tomb. This curse is the oldest known example of the Phoenician alphabet.

Greece

Greek culture during the time of the Phoenicians can be broken into two periods. The first was the Mycenaean Age, which took place between 1600 BCE and 1100 BCE. The Mycenaean Age is the closest to what we think of as ancient Greece and saw the rise of Athens, Thebes, and other legendary city-states. Trade flourished under the Mycenaeans, as it had under their predecessors the Minoans. The higher classes were immensely wealthy during this time, giving rise to craftsmanship and art creation. It was under the Mycenaeans that **Linear B**, the first Greek writing system, was developed. Deities worshipped during the Mycenaean Age remained part of Greek mythology through the Greek Empire's peak in later centuries.

The second period of Greek history that intersected with Phoenician trade dominance was the Greek Dark Ages, which came after the Late Bronze Age Collapse. Following the Late Bronze Age Collapse, culture in Greece became more localized. Thus, each city-state took on its own traditions and styles. Large-scale projects, such as large buildings or wall painting, were not undertaken during this time. Trade became less frequent. Writing stopped among all but the highest

This fresco was created by Greek Minoans on Santorini shortly after the Phoenicians became prominent regional traders.

elites, and many villages were abandoned completely. It was during this time that the Greek theory of **polis**, or independence, was solidified. This development set the stage for the democratic form of governance that we know the civilization for today.

The Greek Dark Ages lasted until around 800 BCE, by which time archaeological evidence suggests city-states were recovering. This was also around the same time that Phoenician trade reached its height, suggesting a connection between the regional recovery from the Late Bronze Age Collapse and flourishing Mediterranean trade.

Mesopotamia

Mesopotamia, in the modern Middle East, was one of the greatest and most culturally important civilizations of the ancient world. During the Phoenician period, it was held by numerous dynasties and empires, beginning with the Old Assyrian period from the sixteenth to the eleventh centuries BCE. The Assyrians were defeated by the Kassites of Babylon in 1595 BCE. In the eleventh century BCE, the Hittites ruled the area.

During the period before the Late Bronze Age Collapse, Mesopotamia made significant advances in mathematics and science, as well as in literature and writing. The Babylonian numeral system became the basis for many measurements still in use today, including the twenty-four-hour day and sixty-minute hour. The libraries of Mesopotamia were among the most celebrated and important of the ancient world. A great deal of literature was translated across languages, such as the extinct Sumerian language. Men and women could read, which made their culture unique among ancient civilizations.

Ancient Mesopotamians were among the first to create codes of law, including the legendary Code of Hammurabi, which was written around 1780 BCE. Under these laws and those that followed, historians have found a gradual move toward restriction of women's rights and a worsening in treatment of slaves. Power was held tightly by hereditary kings who were believed to be gods. In the home, men held all authority. Although Mesopotamian cities were city-states, they all paid taxes to the ruling authority.

The Late Bronze Age Collapse took place in phases across Mesopotamia. In the north, Assyria remained largely intact, with a strong central government and an effective military. Babylon, however, was overrun by invading forces, including Aramaeans and Suteans. These invasions meant that there are few recordings of this time period from city-states across Mesopotamia.

But the collapse's impact was short lived, perhaps due in part to the continued strength of the Assyrians. In the late tenth century BCE, Assyrian king Adad-nirari II conquered Mesopotamia, starting the Neo-Assyrian Empire. That empire would eventually become the largest mankind had ever seen. It encompassed Egypt in the southwest, Iran in the east, and moved up into modern-day Russia in the north. The Neo-Assyrian Empire stood from 911 BCE to 605 BCE, falling to the Neo-Babylonian Empire, which began growing in around 620 BCE.

Although they were largely independent, during this time many Phoenician city-states were part of the Neo-Assyrian Empire. Assyrian control was not constant. However, kings like Tiglath-Pileser III and Ashurbanipal took control of cities like Tyre and Sidon. Control of Phoenician trade ports brought in a great deal of revenue for the Assyrian Empire. Surprisingly, it did not impact Phoenician trade or Phoenician culture significantly.

Egypt

The Phoenician trade routes were established during Egypt's New Kingdom, which dated from 1550 BCE to 1077 BCE. The New Kingdom period is

Queen Hatshepsut of Egypt reigned over one of the empire's most prosperous times and created strong trade relations with regional powers.

commonly called the Egyptian Empire. It was one of the most well-known phases of Egyptian history. The period encompassed the eighteenth, nineteenth, and twentieth dynasties, ending with the death of Pharaoh Ramesses XI in 1069.

During the eighteenth dynasty, some of the best-known pharaohs ruled Egypt, including Hatshepsut, Thutmose III, and Tutankhamen. It was a time of strength and stability for Egypt, with a great deal of power held by priests and religious leaders. The nineteenth dynasty, ushered in by Ramesses II, was marked by expansion. Under Ramesses II and his successors, Egyptian territory grew significantly in the east and south. But political intrigue at court weakened the tight hold on power enjoyed by pharaohs during the eighteenth dynasty.

During the twentieth dynasty, environmental factors and invasion from the Sea Peoples contributed to the Late Bronze Age Collapse. Pharaoh Ramesses III's reign lasted from 1186 BCE to 1155 BCE. During this time, the Sea Peoples attacked Egypt. Although Ramesses III defeated the Sea Peoples and made them subjects, the cost of the two battles on both land and sea led to an economic downturn. Around 1140 BCE, environmental issues that could have been caused by a volcanic eruption caused diminished sunlight. Food shortages soon followed. Food rationing and labor strikes further undermined central authority.

After the death of Ramesses III in 1155 BCE, his sons fought over control of Egypt. The existing food shortages escalated into famine due to droughts, fueling civil unrest. Shortly after Ramesses XI took the throne in 1107, Egypt was effectively divided into Upper, Middle, and Lower Egypt. All were ruled by **de facto leaders**. His death in 1070 BCE marked the end of the New Kingdom and the beginning of the Third Intermediate Period. This was a time of unrest and decline for Egypt.

The Third Intermediate Period dates from 1069 BCE to 664 BCE, making it the primary period during which Phoenician trade routes were active. The period was marked by instability. Foreign invasion was common and power shifted away from kings to priests. The former empire was divided between warring rulers, and new kingdoms were established across Egypt. Between 1100 BCE and 700 BCE, Assyria replaced Egypt as the leading civilization of the Near East. In 670 BCE, Assyria invaded. In the mid-600s BCE, Psamtik I ushered in a period of stability that lasted for nearly a century. But the rise of the Persian Empire threatened the reunited Egypt, and in 525 BCE the Persian king Cambyses II defeated Psamtik III to become pharaoh of Egypt.

Anatolia

Anatolia, which covered much of modern-day Turkey, was ruled by the Hittites from around 1600 BCE to 1180 BCE. Prior to Hittite control, Anatolia was controlled by the Akkadians and the Assyrians. Both cultures were based in Mesopotamia. The Hittites, on the other hand, centered their empire in Anatolia. Their capital was at Hattusa, which was established as their seat of power in around 2000 BCE. The empire they established, called the Hittite Old Kingdom, would eventually control most of Anatolia, or Asia Minor.

Anatolia, in modern Turkey, was a powerful civilization during ancient times. Anatolian art, like this figure, influenced Phoenician art because Anatolians traded with the Phoenician city-states often.

Although there is some debate about who the first king of the Hittite Empire was, most accounts consider Labarna I as the founder of the Old Kingdom. He was the son of PU-Sarruma, about whom we know nearly nothing other than the fact that he was an early pre-empire king of the Hittites. "Labarna" went on to become a title for Hittite kings, leading to some

Herodotus on Phoenician Trade

Herodotus is one of the most celebrated historians of the ancient world, and he lived between 484 BCE and 425 BCE. Here, he writes about the role of Phoenician traders in feuds between the Greeks and the Persians, including the capture of Io, the daughter of a Greek king:

> According to the Persians best informed in history, the Phoenicians began to quarrel ... They landed at many places on the coast, and among the rest at Argos, which was then preeminent above all the states included now under the common name of Hellas. Here they exposed their merchandise, and traded with the natives for five or six days; at the end of which time, when almost everything was sold, there came down to the beach a number of women, and among them the daughter of the king, who was, they say, agreeing in this with the Greeks, Io, the child of Inachus. The women were standing by the stern of the ship intent upon their purchases, when the Phoenicians, with a general shout, rushed upon them. The greater part made their escape, but some were seized and carried off. Io herself was among the captives. The Phoenicians put the women on board their vessel, and set sail for Egypt. Thus did Io pass into Egypt, according to the Persian story, which differs widely from the Phoenician: and thus commenced, according to their authors, the series of outrages.

Herodotus was a Greek historian who wrote frequently about trade with Phoenicia, giving us some of the only accounts of the civilization.

confusion over the naming of other rulers. Under Labarna I, his successor Hattusili I (also sometimes called Labarna II), and Mursili I, the Hittites waged wars of conquest against the Levant and Mesopotamia.

Under Mursili I, the Hittites took control of Yamhad. This was a region of northern Syria with the capital of Aleppo. In 1531 BCE, Mursili I attacked Babylon. It was the farthest south a Hittite ruler had taken his army at that time. Although he did not conquer Babylon, historians believe it did end the rule of the Amorite dynasty and made space for the Kassites to take control.

Mursili I was assassinated in a coup when he returned to Anatolia. His death ushered in a period of unrest that eventually led into the Late Bronze Age Collapse. Under his successors, the Old Kingdom experienced civil unrest and a loss of central control. The Assyrians retook control of the territories in Syria that Mursili I had claimed. Little is known of this period of Hittite rule due to poor records and a rapid succession of rulers. Zidanta I followed Mursili's successor. He ruled only for ten years before being killed by his son, Ammuna, who took the throne after his father's death. It was during Ammuna's reign that most of the Hittite territory outside of Anatolia was lost. Ammuna fought wars against cities that may have been in rebellion.

The trend of assassinations and unrest continued until the early fourteenth century BCE, when Tudhaliya I ushered in what is called the New Kingdom. Tudhaliya I strengthened central rule and expanded settlements while establishing good relations with neighboring peoples. He also reclaimed Aleppo in northern Syria and spread Hittite rule west. His successors lost and gained territory over the centuries, until 1180 BCE. Then the Late Bronze Age Collapse caused the dissolution of the Hittite Empire.

During the Late Bronze Age Collapse, the Hittite Empire was attacked and conquered by the Arameans, Luwians, and Phrygians. The Hittite capital at Hattusa was destroyed. Their territory was divided into smaller, independent states. Shortly thereafter, the Assyrian Empire claimed much of the area, with the Phrygians claiming most of the rest. For the rest of antiquity, Anatolia was held by various empires. First it was absorbed by Rome, and then it became the seat of the Byzantine Empire.

Chapter 5

The Effects of the Phoenician Trade Routes

The effect Phoenician trade routes had on the culture, politics, religion, and economy of the Mediterranean was wide ranging and significant. The goods and services the Phoenicians traded in shaped the way cultures interpreted social status, access to reading and writing, the way people worshipped, and what they knew about the world around them. The Phoenicians also expanded the reach of the Mediterranean empires through expansion of their trade routes, reaching into modern Spain, Africa, and possibly western Europe. In those interactions, they brought Mediterranean traditions to indigenous people, introducing them to

Opposite: *This tablet in modern Libya shows Latin and Phoenician, two of the world's most influential alphabets.*

elaborate rituals that had been confined to the region but eventually influenced the way power was defined across the ancient world.

The Phoenicians also played another crucial role in the ancient Mediterranean, assisting in recovery from the Late Bronze Age Collapse and helping cultures bridge the Bronze Age and the Iron Age. Phoenician technology in ship making, navigation, writing, and the arts helped push mankind forward, ushering in adaptations on their ideas that came to define the civilizations with which they interacted. Although not the largest or most powerful force in their time, the Phoenicians were an influential and crucial piece of the regional and global system that evolved in the second and first millennia BCE.

In this chapter, we will learn more about the way the Phoenicians shaped the ancient world and the lasting legacy of their trade routes. We'll explore the way trade helped move mankind forward, influence the empires of the Mediterranean, and lay the foundation on which those empires rose in the wake of the Late Bronze Age Collapse.

The Late Bronze Age Collapse

As previously mentioned, the Late Bronze Age Collapse was a catastrophic wave of destruction, famine, and invasion that left the empires of the Mediterranean weakened and divided. In Greece, Egypt, Mesopotamia, and Anatolia, the mysterious and complex combination of foreign wars, food shortages, political infighting, and natural disaster led to the destruction of major cities. These factors also caused the loss of central authority and a disruption in what had been widespread cultural advancement. Over the course of about one century between 1200 BCE and 1100 BCE, each of these empires experienced setbacks that threatened their survival and could have changed the course of history.

Yet Phoenicia was largely unimpacted. This could be due to a few reasons. Evidence exists that the Sea Peoples, who invaded and destroyed cities in Egypt and Mesopotamia, allied with the Phoenicians. While cities and villages were being abandoned and destroyed across the ancient world, Phoenician cities were untouched. This could also be due to the small size of Phoenicia and the independent nature of its city-states, which made it easier for city-states to hold territory. The Phoenicians were also not an agricultural people. They lived in an area of the Levant without arable land. As such, crops the Phoenicians grew were able to thrive in adverse climates, making them resilient and able to stand up to environmental changes of that time. Regardless of why they were not impacted significantly, the Phoenicians were well placed to make the most of the suddenly cleared field of the Mediterranean. They filled a **vacuum** that was left when other civilizations retreated.

The Late Bronze Age Collapse opened a unique opportunity for the small Phoenician city-states to take advantage of established trade routes. The Assyrians and the Mycenaeans had dominated trade in the Mediterranean and Middle East prior to the Late Bronze Age Collapse. This means that there were established land and limited sea routes that the Phoenicians could use as a foundation for the much more expansive trade network they built over the course of centuries.

Trade brought great wealth to the Phoenicians, but it also helped the empires surrounding them recover from the Late Bronze Age Collapse. Phoenician trade routes expanded gradually, creating networks of communication and economic cooperation across civilizations. Access to raw materials, like wood or metals, helped cultures kick-start their stagnant building and cultural undertakings. Phoenicia was also able to create exchanges of low-value goods for high-value goods. They essentially used supply and demand to ensure empires and civilizations had access to goods they needed in exchange for those they had in excess. In this way, trade was a crucial part of the rebound following the Late Bronze Age Collapse. Trade helped usher in stability and growth for many of the civilizations in the Mediterranean.

The Bronze Age vs. the Iron Age

Phoenician trade routes grew during a time of profound change in the ancient world. The Bronze Age lasted from 3300 BCE to around 1200 BCE in the East and around 3200 BCE to 600 BCE in Europe. It came to an end as the Phoenicians were becoming a trade power. This gave way to the Iron Age, which spanned from 1200 BCE to 500 BCE in the East and 1200 BCE to 1 BCE in Europe. The shift was gradual but important. It marked large changes in the way people lived, waged wars, created art, and interacted with the world around them.

The Bronze Age ended slowly. Some cultures adapted to iron-based weaponry and technology more quickly than others. This gave them an advantage in warfare, allowing once small cultures to claim territory from larger powers, such as the Hittites. The Assyrians also lost ground to opponents fighting with iron. However, they eventually went on to reclaim their dominance in the Middle East. Iron also allowed for widespread changes in agriculture, with tools that were more efficient and stronger than prior bronze tools.

The Iron Age ushered in other changes in culture, such as shifts in artistic styles, architecture, and power dynamics. The Phoenicians were dominant in the metal trade. Thus, their role was important and complex as the use of bronze gave way to the use of iron. Iron, tin, and copper (the latter two used to make bronze) were some of Phoenicia's largest trade commodities. These metals were traded in raw forms and used to make goods in Phoenicia before export. The hunt for iron also led to Phoenician expansion. Iberia became a key source for the important metal.

The period of Phoenician trade dominance overlapped with the period of transition between the late Bronze Age and the early Iron Age. In a way, this overlap means that the Phoenicians were trading with partners in two different time periods. This is particularly true considering that the Phoenicians had trade partners outside of the Mediterranean and in Europe, where the Bronze Age did not end until 600 BCE. As one of the driving forces of cross-cultural exchange in that time, the Phoenicians played an indirect but important role in helping cultures shape each other.

Culture

The Phoenicians had a significant impact on the culture of the Mediterranean, as we've discussed in previous chapters. From writing to social status to art, the Phoenicians facilitated cultural changes.They did so through both their own exported goods and through communication between far-spread areas of the ancient world. The cultural influence of Phoenician trade included everything from religion to clothing. It had a lasting impact throughout the centuries, even after the Phoenicians were no longer the dominant traders in the region.

One of the most significant examples of the cultural influence of the Phoenicians is their presence in the writings of other civilizations. Across the ancient world, and most notably in the works of Homer and Herodotus, we're given a secondhand view of how other people saw the Phoenicians.

In his *Histories*, Herodotus writes about the role of Phoenicia in shaping trade relationships that came to define the ancient world. In Book I, he says:

> The Phoenicians, who had formerly dwelt on the shores of the Persian Gulf, having migrated to the Mediterranean and settled in the parts which they now inhabit, began at once, they say, to adventure on long voyages, freighting their vessels with the wares of Egypt and Assyria.

Herodotus also wrote about the Phoenician alphabet being introduced to the Greeks in Book V:

> These Phoenicians who came with Cadmus and of whom the Gephyraeans were a part brought with them to Hellas, among many other kinds of learning, the alphabet, which had been unknown before this, I

Harbors like this one in Sidon were the heart of Phoenician trade. Great cities were built around them.

> think, to the Greeks. As time went on the sound and the form of the letters were changed. At this time the Greeks who were settled around them were for the most part Ionians, and after being taught the letters by the Phoenicians, they used them with a few changes of form. In so doing, they gave to these characters the name of Phoenician.

Yet Herodotus was not the only writer to refer to the Phoenicians. In the *Odyssey* and the *Iliad*, Homer frequently mentions the Phoenicians. Most notably, for Homer the Phoenicians were both cunning traders and able to produce luxurious goods of high value. In the *Odyssey*, he refers to them as, "The famous sea-dogs, sharp bargainers too, the holds of their black ship brimful with a hoard of flashy baubles."

In the *Iliad*, the Phoenicians appear again, this time as the source of an unparalleled silver bowl:

> For the next event, the quarter mile, Achilles offered a silver winebowl of six gallons. Never a mixing bowl in all the world could match its beauty: artisans of Sidon had lavished art upon it. Phoenicians had brought it by sea and, mooring ship in a roadstead, had conferred the bowl on Thoas Euneos, son of Jason, later gave it as ransom to Patroclos for Lykaon, son of Priam. Now at his old friend's funeral Achilles put the bowl down, as first prize, for that man who should prove the faster runner.

Technology

Technology was a huge part of the Phoenician trade network. Technological and scientific advances in ship making and navigation gave Phoenician traders an advantage in the harsh Mediterranean. This allowed them to expand their network beyond any established before their time. As discussed previously, Phoenicians developed two types of ships that helped them master the seas. Phoenician galloi ships were tub-like and rounded, sitting higher in the water with weights in the back and protected storage holds for cargo. These ships featured oars for steering and a loose hanging sail that could catch the wind from any direction.

Their warships featured a metal spike on the hull that could be used to ram other ships, as well as oars and a decorative horse head that adorned each end. These ships would go on to influence Greek and Roman ship making. The Phoenicians' discovery of the North Star and navigation methods also helped make sea travel more reliable and safe.

Our understanding of Phoenician ships comes from artistic representations, records of Egyptians and other empires with which the Phoenicians traded, and shipwrecks discovered around the Mediterranean. The Balawat Gate, built around 850 BCE, depicts Phoenician ships bearing timber and metal. The Greek writer Xenophon tells us that the ships were extremely efficient in terms of how they were laid out:

> I think that the best and most perfect arrangement of things that I ever saw was when I went to look at the great Phoenician sailing-vessel; for I saw the largest amount of naval tackling separately disposed in the smallest stowage possible. For a ship, as you well know, is brought to anchor, and again got under way, by a vast number of wooden implements and of ropes and sails the sea by means of a quantity of rigging, and is armed with a number of contrivances against hostile vessels, and carries about with it a large supply of weapons for the crew, and, besides, has all the utensils that a man keeps in his dwelling-house, for each of the messes. In addition, it is laden with

> a quantity of merchandise which the owner carries with him for his own profit. Now all the things which I have mentioned lay in a space not much bigger than a room which would conveniently hold ten beds.

Shipwrecks have been key to our understanding of Phoenician trade, giving us a look at what goods ships carried, how ships were built, and how relations played out between traders and trade partners. Shipwrecks have provided historians with concrete examples of the artwork traded throughout the ancient world, including ivory tusks and stone altars. They also provide a look at how the crew lived. According to historian Michael Polzer, who examined a shipwreck at Bajo de la Campana, the wreck was remarkable for one specific reason:

> One of the puzzling aspects of this shipwreck excavation was that we found very few objects that can be categorized as shipboard equipment or personal effects of the crew. Whetstones and pan-balance weights are best interpreted as belonging to a craftsman or merchant on board the vessel, and the charring around the nozzles of the only intact lamp we recovered indicates that it was used aboard the ship. But there is little else that speaks to the Phoenician sailors themselves.

The lack of personal effects could be due to the use of trade posts and colonies, which allowed ships to travel primarily by day rather than take long multiday journeys. Sailing primarily by daylight made it possible for Phoenician sailors to keep the coastline in view. This was a simple and effective method of navigation that helped protect their wares from threats, such as pirates.

Colonies

Colonies were one of the most direct lasting legacies of the Phoenician trade routes. Phoenicia was not a military power in the sense of larger empires. As such, Phoenicia did not conquer outlying areas in order to set up colonies. Instead, the Phoenicians established small outposts and cities along their trade routes. These functioned as markets, factories, and stopping-off points for ships. Some of them went on to be powers in their own right. Some remain important cities today.

It is unclear when colonization started, due in part to the fact that many colonies remained small and eventually vanished. Like Phoenician trade routes, Phoenician colonial growth was focused on the south Mediterranean and mirrored Greek colonization in the north. Some accounts seem to speak of colonies as early as the twelfth and tenth centuries BCE. Yet the first physical evidence of Phoenician colonies dates them to around the eighth century BCE.

The first Phoenician colonies were small outposts on the coast. They had shallow harbors ideal for use as ports. Some of these developed more permanent structures and markets, becoming regional trading powers capable of expanding Phoenician trade deeper into Africa and Europe. Colonies were used as production sites for Tyrian dye, glass, and other goods the Phoenicians were famous for producing. Many became sources of goods like metals and food. Slaves were also captured from the areas around the colonies or sold to traders at the outpost markets.

Because the Phoenicians were not interested in conquering the indigenous people of any given area, they were able to develop interesting relationships with those surrounding their colonies. Iberia, for instance, had previously not had relations with the empires of the Mediterranean. Phoenicians brought gifts and offerings traditionally given to the rulers of Egypt or Mesopotamia there. This introduced new practices and goods to these cultures, creating cross-cultural exchange through trade. It also allowed the Phoenicians to carry out their ultimate goal: establishing relationships that allowed them to gain access to goods, services, and markets wherever they could.

Diodorus of Sicily wrote in the first century BCE about Malta's founding as a Phoenician colony:

> It possesses many harbours which offer exceptional advantage, and its inhabitants are blest in their possessions; for it has artisans skilled in every manner of craft... and the dwellings on the island are worthy of note, being ambitiously constructed with cornices and finishes in stucco with unusual workmanship. The island is a colony planted by the Phoenicians, who, as they extended their trade in the western ocean, found in it a place of safe retreat, since it was well supplied with harbours and lay

> out in the open sea; and this is the reason why the inhabitants of this island, since they received assistance in many respects through the sea-merchants, shot up quickly in their manner of living and increased in renown.

The people of Tyre, Sidon, and Byblos were among the most active colonizers of Phoenicia. The Phoenicians established colonies along their Mediterranean trade routes, from Cyprus as early as the eleventh century BCE to Iberia in the tenth century BCE. Carthage, as discussed in previous chapters, is one of the most famous and important colonies established by the Phoenicians. It enjoyed growth and prosperity, as well as popular support. In 340 BCE, Aristotle wrote about Carthage:

> The Carthaginians are also considered to have an excellent form of government, which differs from that of any other state in several respects, though it is in some very like the Spartan. Indeed, all three states—the Spartan, the Cretan, and the Carthaginian—nearly resemble one another, and are very different from any others. Many of the Carthaginian institutions are excellent. The superiority of their constitution is proved by the fact that the common people remain loyal to the constitution. The Carthaginians have never had any rebellion worth speaking of, and have never been under the rule of a tyrant.

Punic Wars

Carthage was ruled by a series of monarchs. (According to legend, Queen Dido was the first.) Under the monarchs' leadership, Carthage grew into a powerful empire after Phoenicia lost dominance in the region. But Carthage clashed with Rome numerous times, including during the three Punic Wars. This series of conflicts took place between 264 BCE and 146 BCE. The Punic Wars are considered by historians to be some of the largest seen at that point in history.

The wars were fought over rivalry for territory, as both empires expanded into the Mediterranean and Iberia. The First Punic War was fought between 264 BCE and 241 BCE, spanning both land and sea. It began when the Mamertines on Sicily asked for Carthaginian assistance against a local aggressor. The Carthaginians arrived and built a garrison to help. Yet the Mamertines betrayed them and called on the Romans to help fight against Carthage. In the Second Punic War, fought on land between 218 BCE and 201 BCE, the Carthaginian commander Hannibal famously rode elephants over the Alps. The Third Punic War, between 149 BCE and 146 BCE, was a thorough defeat of Carthage at the hands of Rome. It involved a prolonged siege of the city and its eventual destruction.

Hannibal brought elephants over the Alps to fight Rome. He is one of Carthage's most famous rulers.

Carthage was a coastal colony of Phoenicia that became an important kingdom after Phoenicia lost independence.

Others, such as Ebusus (Ibiza), Panormo (Palermo), and Hippo Diarrhytus (Bizerte), went on to become cities in the modern era. Although Phoenician religion and trade were a large part of the lives of those who lived in these colonies, the local culture also influenced the way Phoenicia developed. These outposts were truly the best examples of how Phoenicia interacted with the world.

Trade Expansion

The Phoenicians didn't invent large-scale regional trade; they made use of existing trade routes. But what they did accomplish was expanding the scope of trade across the ancient world. From China in the East to Britain and Africa in the West, Phoenician traders created what could be called one of the world's first global economic networks. Some historians believe the Phoenicians may have reached South America. However, there is little evidence of this beyond inscriptions.

While focused primarily on economic opportunity, the Phoenicians were some of the most efficient and successful explorers of their age. They connected parts of the world that had previously not been in contact and shared knowledge among populations.

The Phoenicians expanded the understanding of the world and shaped the way empires thought about themselves in relation to others. In the centuries after Phoenicia came under Persian control, the Greek Empire fell and the Roman Empire was established. The Roman Empire grew into one of the greatest powers the world had ever seen. But the world they conquered, from west to east, was one first connected by the Phoenicians.

Chapter 6

The End of the Phoenician Trade Routes

Phoenician trade routes thrived for almost one thousand years before effectively ending in 539 BCE. That year, Cyrus the Great brought Phoenicia and the rest of the Near East under Persian rule. Then, starting in 334 BCE, Alexander the Great brought Phoenicia under Macedonian rule after two centuries of fighting between Persia and the Greek kingdom of Macedon. The end of Phoenician trade was gradual. Pressures from a series of invading forces made it difficult for the city-states to maintain the independence they once had. Taxes and tributes also put strain on the local economy. Meanwhile, the Phoenicians were unable to maintain sole control over the routes they established. Colonies like Carthage broke away and became powers in their own right.

Opposite: *Alexander the Great expanded the Macedonian Kingdom to include most of the known world, including Phoenicia.*

As the Common Era neared, Rome replaced Phoenicia as the dominant trader of the Mediterranean. The Persians came to dominate most of East Asia. Phoenicia, although not destroyed completely, adapted and its people assimilated as the centuries went on. Phoenicians eventually lost the distinct identity that set them apart from other regional populations. It was a quiet end for a small civilization that shaped its own era.

In this chapter, we will look at the empires that absorbed Phoenicia and how they changed the way the city-states functioned. We will also learn about Cyrus the Great and Alexander the Great, two of the ancient world's greatest leaders who each played a role in the downfall of Phoenicia. Finally, we will look at Phoenicia under Roman rule and how Phoenician identity changed over the centuries.

Assyrian Rule

Phoenicia rested on the edge of Mesopotamia, and so its city-states came under control of the empires ruling the area from time to time. Assyria was no exception. From around 883 BCE the Neo-Assyrian Empire held power over Phoenicia for stretches of time. Phoenicia was not a military power. As such, it did not engage in traditional warfare when it was possible to avoid it.

Neo-Assyrian rulers, beginning with Ashurnasirpal II in 883 BCE, did not seek to conquer Phoenicia but rather to get the leaders of each city-state to pay them tribute in goods and precious metals. Ashurnasirpal II himself wrote about receiving tributes from the Phoenicians: "The tribute of the sea coast—from the inhabitants of Tyre, Sidon, Byblos, Mahallata,

The Assyrians were often in conflict with Middle Eastern powers as they sought to conquer the region, including Phoenicia.

Kaiza, Amurru and Arvad which is an Island in the sea, consisting of gold, silver, tin, copper, copper-containers, linen garments with multi-colored trimmings, large and small monkeys, ebony, boxwood, ivory from walrus tusk, a product of the sea—this their tribute I received and they embraced my feet."

Between 883 BCE and 605 BCE, Phoenicia alternated between paying tribute to Assyrian kings and rebelling against their rule. The rulers themselves were far more concerned with threats from Egypt, Babylon, and other forces seeking to claim their territory. They left Phoenicia to function largely independently. These conflicts and a series of revolts from within their territory weakened the Assyrians to the point of defeat. Around 605 BCE the empire fell to the Babylonians.

Phoenicia briefly fell to the Babylonian Empire, but the Persians under Cyrus the Great soon defeated them. This Babylonian painting is part of the University of Chicago's collection.

The Babylonian Empire was short lived and saw numerous rebellions. Babylon ruled Phoenicia from 605 BCE to 539 BCE. Rebellions were common under Nabopolassar. They were also common under his son, the famed king Nebuchadnezzar. Rebellions even occurred in the Phoenician city-states, including a thirteen-year uprising in Tyre that ended with a long siege. Babylon would later fall to the Persian leader Cyrus the Great.

Persian Rule

Cyrus the Great came to power in 559 BCE during the Achaemenid dynasty. He became one of ancient Persia's greatest leaders. During his thirty-year reign, Cyrus conquered the Median, Lydian, and Babylonian empires, as well as large parts of the Far East. In the lands he controlled, Cyrus put in place a system of government that respected local values, religions, and norms. He left behind what the United Nations has called an ancient declaration of human rights. In a book called the *Cyropaedia*, Greek historian Xenophon wrote: "And those who were subject to him, he treated with esteem and regard, as if they were his own children, while his subjects themselves respected Cyrus as their 'Father.'"

Cyrus conquered the Babylonian Empire in around 539 BCE, taking control of the Phoenician city-states and the rest of the Near East. He split Phoenicia into smaller kingdoms, centered on Sidon, Tyre, Arwad, and Byblos. For about two centuries the kingdoms thrived. They used their ship-making skills to provide fleets for Persian rulers. They also fought with the Persians against the Greeks in the Greco-Persian Wars of the early 400s BCE.

Cyrus the Great was one of Persia's most famed rulers, conquering large territories and bringing wealth and prestige to the empire.

But Persian rule of Phoenicia was brief, lasting only a handful of centuries. Cyrus was a just and loved ruler and Persia was one of the great civilizations of the ancient world. However, his successors were less successful at holding together the empire he built. In 465 BCE, King Xerxes I was killed by a Persian guard and official. Artaxerxes took the throne. Under him, Egypt revolted against Persian rule, marking the beginning of significant unrest in the empire. The kings who reigned after Artaxerxes faced a terribly high risk of assassination. Some served for only a handful of days before being killed by rivals. Meanwhile, rebellions began taking place in Phoenicia. In Sidon, a rebellion around 350 BCE resulted in the city's destruction at the hands of King Artaxerxes III.

Weakened by war in Egypt and Greece and by rebellions, the Achaemenid Persian Empire fell in 300 BCE to Alexander the Great, a Macedonian ruler.

Alexander the Great

Alexander the Great ruled Macedon, a Greek kingdom, from 336 BCE to 323 BCE. In that time, he conquered much of the known world, including Egypt, Persia, and much of the Far East. Under Alexander, Greek culture spread throughout the ancient world. He remains one of the most celebrated military strategists in human history. Yet while Cyrus took Phoenicia with relative ease, Alexander showed a brutality that effectively destroyed the city of Tyre, one of the most important cities in Phoenician trade.

Alexander inherited the throne from his father, Philip. Soon after taking power, he began working to expand his territory and strengthen the grip his father had on Macedonian holdings. Historian Plutarch, who wrote one of the first memorials of Alexander, writes:

> Thus it was that at the age of twenty years Alexander received the kingdom, which was

> exposed to great jealousies, dire hatreds, and dangers on every hand. For the neighbouring tribes of Barbarians would not tolerate their servitude, and longed for their hereditary kingdoms; and as for Greece, although Philip had conquered her in the field, he had not had time enough to make her tame under his yoke, but had merely disturbed and changed the condition of affairs there, and then left them in a great surge and commotion, owing to the strangeness of the situation. The Macedonian counsellors of Alexander had fears of the crisis, and thought he should give up the Greek states altogether and use no more compulsion there, and that he should call the revolting Barbarians back to their allegiance by mild measures and try to arrest the first symptoms of their revolutions; but he himself set out from opposite principles to win security and safety for his realm by boldness and a lofty spirit, assured that, were he seen to abate his dignity even but a little, all his enemies would set upon him.

In 333 BCE, Alexander launched a campaign to claim the Near East from Persia, then ruled by Darius III. Despite being outnumbered, he succeeded. Yet not all his new territory came quietly. The people of Tyre refused to surrender to him. After a long siege, Alexander defeated the rebellion there. Upon claiming Tyre, he killed all the men and sold the surviving women and children into slavery. This brought a temporary end to Phoenicia's leading trade city.

Tyre

Tyre had an important place in Phoenician history, as both an economic power and a strongly independent city-state. It was where Tyrian dye, one of Phoenicia's most lucrative and iconic exports, was produced. Tyre also founded Carthage,

Tyre was one of the most successful Phoenician city-states, and its people often rebelled against conquering powers.

one of the most legendary of Phoenicia's colonies. Tyre's history is littered with sieges, rebellions, destructions, and massacres. Yet the city was always rebuilt. Following the reign of the Macedonians and the Seleucids, Tyre became semi-independent under the Romans. The Romans granted it the status of *civitas foederata*, or an ally rather than a subject state. It regained its footing as a commercial center over the centuries. The city appeared in the Bible and became the site of remarkable structures. After revolting against Byzantine rule in the first millennia CE, it became part of the Kingdom of Jerusalem. Then it was brought under Ottoman rule in the 1200s CE.

In modern day, Tyre is one of the largest cities in Lebanon, a coastal country in the Middle East. Today, tourism is the largest industry due to the Roman Hippodrome located there, which is a UNESCO World Heritage Site. Despite being destroyed numerous times throughout its history, Tyre remains an important part of the regional system of cities and communities. It is a testament to the continuity of history.

After the destruction of Tyre, the rest of the Phoenician city-states surrendered quietly. Macedon's rise brought about the end of the Phoenician trade routes. As Macedonian and Roman traders began taking control of the Mediterranean, the Phoenicians struggled with a succession of new rulers, tributes, and rebellions. Under Alexander, Greek culture and to some extent Persian culture replaced Phoenicia's distinct identity. However, colonies like Carthage remained independent and played a role in trade for years to come.

The End of Phoenicia

After being conquered by Alexander the Great, Phoenicia would never again be independent in the way it was during the height of its role in trade. The territory passed from the Macedonians to the Seleucid dynasty, then came under Roman rule. The Romans governed the area that was once Phoenicia as a province called Phoenice. Sidon, Byblos, and even Tyre once again began exporting goods like wine, wood, and glass. But this trade was not for their own gain. Their profits now fed the growing Roman Empire, which controlled the trade routes of the Mediterranean. The empire had conquered the world the Phoenicians connected centuries before. Eventually, the area became part of the Byzantine Empire, then the Ottoman Empire, and finally modern Lebanon.

Today our limited knowledge of Phoenicia makes it something of a mystery. The area where it once stood has been continuously inhabited since ancient history. Therefore, excavation of important Phoenician sites is nearly impossible. What we do know comes from second-hand reports from neighboring states, historical accounts of those who came later. We also have limited artifacts historians have discovered, including shipwrecks and some port cities. The picture this evidence paints is of a complex, cunning, and opportunistic people able to seize a moment in history that was unique in the ancient world. Phoenicians used the vacuum created by the Late Bronze Age Collapse to grow into a power in their own right.

In the years that followed, trade continued to play a vital role in the Mediterranean. The region was dominated first by the Roman Empire, then the Muslim Caliphate of the early Common Era, and finally the Ottoman Empire. The foundation of much of that trade was laid by the Phoenicians. Those who came after them built on the trade routes and traditions started by the small Levant civilization.

But despite the near erasure of the Phoenicians, their legacy outlasted them by millennia. In art styles and alphabets, symbolic colors and wine, Phoenicians shaped the world in which they lived to the extent that history would be unrecognizable without them. They explored the known world and connected empires, discovered new ways to navigate the seas and built ships in which to do so, and found their way into the works of great writers. Although few people know about the Phoenicians, we see their shadow and influence throughout history. We have their trade routes to thank.

Glossary

bureaucracies The officials and organizations of states, including institutions and regulations.

city-states Cities that function as independent countries.

civilizations Ways of life in an area or individual society.

coup The violent overthrow of an established government.

cross-cultural Having to do with the sharing of goods or ideas across the boundaries of culture, state, or empire.

de facto leaders Those who take power unofficially.

deities Gods or beings that are worshipped.

hereditary monarchy A ruling system in which power passes within the same family from one generation to the next.

hierarchy The way status is ranked in a society, group, or other institution. Those at the top of the hierarchy are the most powerful, while those at the bottom are the least powerful.

imperial aspirations Goals relating to building an empire or expanding territory.

Linear B The oldest form of the Greek alphabet; Linear B uses more than 187 symbols and signs.

maritime Related to the sea.

mercantile Related to trade.

numerals Any symbols or figures that are used to mean a number.

phonetic An alphabet that uses symbols to represent sounds rather than objects or words.

polis An idealized system of government and the basis for democracy; "polis" can also mean "city-state."

polytheistic Describes religions that include the worship of more than one god.

Semitic Peoples who come from a family of languages that include Hebrew, Arabic, and Aramaic.

status symbols Goods or items that suggest wealth and standing in a society.

vacuum A situation that occurs when there is no dominant power in a political region, allowing for one or multiple states or groups to claim power.

Further Information

Websites

Ancient History Encyclopedia
http://www.ancient.eu
The Ancient History Encyclopedia features a searchable database of articles about the ancient world, including big-picture summaries of Phoenicia and the ancient Mediterranean.

BBC Ancient History
http://www.bbc.com/history/ancient
This wonderful resource from the BBC has articles, pictures, and background information on cultures across the ancient world, like the Assyrians and Egyptians.

The Metropolitan Museum: The Phoenicians
http://www.metmuseum.org/toah/hd/phoe/hd_phoe.htm
The Metropolitan Museum's website focuses on the arts, providing information about trade routes that facilitated cultural exchange and ancient cultures that traded with one another, including Phoenicia and Persia.

The Perseus Project
http://www.perseus.tufts.edu/
Search this online library to find primary source texts, information from experts on Greek and Roman history, and descriptions of Phoenician trade patterns.

Books

Cline, Eric H. *1177 B.C.: The Year Civilization Collapsed.* Princeton, NJ: Princeton University Press, 2014.

Kriwaczek, Paul. *Babylon: Mesopotamia and the Birth of Civilization.* New York, NY: St. Martin's Press, 2010.

Markoe, Glenn. *Phoenicians*. Los Angeles, CA: University of California Press, 2000.

Moscati, Sabatino. *The World of the Phoenicians*. London, UK: Weidenfield & Nicholson, 1999.

Videos

"Mesopotamia: Crash Course World History #3" (2012)
https://youtu.be/sohXPx_XZ6Y
This fast-paced video provides an overview of Mesopotamia that is aligned with high school curriculum.

"The Punic Wars"
http://www.history.com/topics/ancient-history/punic-wars/videos
The History Channel's website features a roundup of short videos about topics like the military strategies Hannibal employed and more.

Bibliography

Aubet, Maria Eugenia. *The Phoenicians and the West: Politics, Colonies, and Trade.* Cambridge, UK: Cambridge University Press, 1994.

Bement, R. B. *Tyre: The History of Phoenicia, Palestine, and Syria*. Charleston, SC: Nabu Press, 2013.

Bierling, Marilyn R. *The Phoenicians in Spain*. Winona Lake, IN: Eisenbrauns, 2002.

Bowersock, Glen Warren, and Walter Miller. *Xenophon*. Boston, MA: Harvard University Press, 1997.

Curtin, Phillip D. *Cross-Cultural Trade in World History*. Cambridge, UK: Cambridge University Press, 1984.

Dewald, Carolyn. *The Histories*. Oxford, UK: Oxford University Press, 2008.

Edwards, I.E.S. *Cambridge Ancient History*. Cambridge, UK: Cambridge University Press, 1924.

Heinemann, W. *Plutarch's Lives, Volume 5*. London, UK: William Heinemann, 1917.

Lewy, Hildegrad. *Cambridge Ancient History: Assyria*. Cambridge, UK: Cambridge University Press, 1966.

Markoe, Glenn. *Phoenicians*. Los Angeles, CA: University of California Press, 2000.

Martin, Thomas R. *Ancient Greece*. Hartford, CT: Yale University Press, 2013.

McIntosh, Jane. *Ancient Mesopotamia: New Perspectives*. Santa Barbara, CA: ABC-CLIO, 2005.

Moscati, Sabatino. *The Phoenicians*. New York, NY: I. B. Tauris, 2001.

Neville, Ann. *Mountains of Silver & Rivers of Gold: The Phoenicians in Iberia*. Oxford, UK: Oxbow Books, 2007.

Oppenheim, A. Leo. *Ancient Mesopotamia: Portrait of a Dead Civilization*. Chicago, IL: University of Chicago Press, 1977.

Quinn, Josephine Crawley, and Nicholas C. Vella. *The Punic Mediterranean: Identities and Identification from Phoenician Settlement to Roman Rule*. Cambridge, UK: Cambridge University Press, 2014.

Rawlinson, George. *Phoenicia: History of a Civilization*. New York, NY: I. B. Tauris, 2005.

Smith, Richard L. *Premodern Trade in World History*. New York, NY: Routledge, 2009.

Yamada, Shigeo. *The Construction of the Assyrian Empire*. Boston, MA: Brill, 2000.

Index

Page numbers in **boldface** are illustrations. Entries in **boldface** are glossary terms.

About the Author

Bridey Heing is a writer and book critic based in Washington, DC. She holds degrees in political science and international affairs from DePaul University and Washington University in Saint Louis. Her areas of focus are comparative politics and Iranian politics. Her master's thesis explores the evolution of populist politics and democracy in Iran since 1900. She has written about Iranian affairs, women's rights, and art and politics for publications like the *Economist*, *Hyperallergic*, and the *Establishment*. She also writes about literature and film. She enjoys traveling, reading, and exploring Washington's many museums.